S0-BNJ-169

THE ROCKER

ISBN 978-1-4234-5632-2

HAL•LEONARD® CORPORATION

7777 W. BLUEMOUND RD. P.O. BOX 13819 MILWAUKEE, WI 53213

Visit Hal Leonard Online at
www.halleonard.com

TOMORROW NEVER COMES

Words and Music by
CHAD FISCHER

Moderate Rock feel

You wake up ___ with the ra-di-o on, ___
Back in the ___ same day once ___ a - gain, ___

and "I Got You Babe" ___ is the same ___ old ___
no con - se - quen - ces in a ___ life ___

To - mor - row nev - er comes.

COMING THROUGH IN STEREO

Words and Music by CHAD FISCHER
and PATRICK HOULIHAN

Uptempo Rock

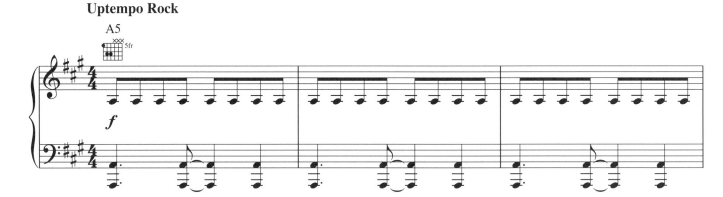

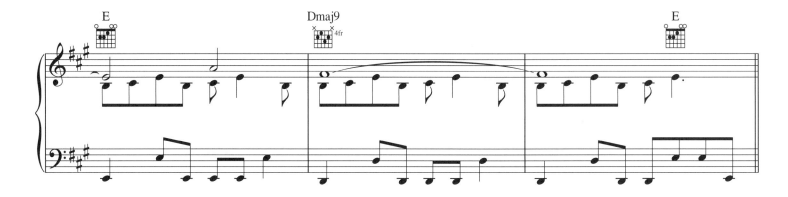

To Coda

coming in strong.__ We're com-ing through in ste - re - o, don't look back 'cause here we go.__

And now you wake up in a brand new__ town,__ and

play that song__ to a brand__ new crowd.__ And with the mel - o - dy, they__

So turn __ up that ra - di - o song,

keep it on while it's com-ing in strong. __ We're com-ing through in ste - re - o,

BITTER

Words and Music by
CHAD FISCHER

Min - utes turn in - to ho -

LIVING FOR THE FIRST TIME

Words and Music by CHRISTOPHER FAIZI
and FERRABY LIONHEART

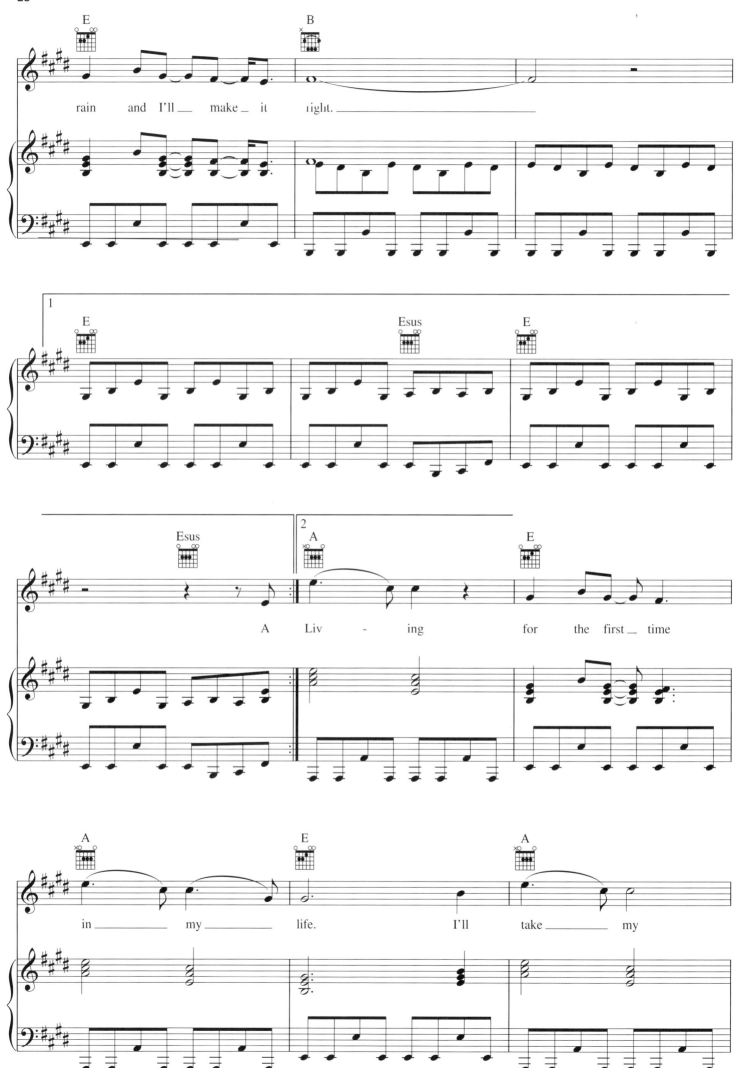

DOWN

Words and Music by FERRABY LIONHEART
and CHRISTOPHER FAIZI

Pop Rock

GREAT ESCAPE

Words and Music by
CHAD FISCHER

D.S. al Coda

NOTHIN' BUT A GOOD TIME

Words and Music by BOBBY DALL, BRETT MICHAELS,
BRUCE JOHANNESSON and RIKKI ROCKETT

Energetic Rock

Ooh. _____

Not a dime, _ I can't pay my _ rent, _ I can
spend _ my _ mon-ey on _ wom-en and wine, _ but

bare-ly make it through _ the week. _____
I _____ could-n't tell you where I _ spent last night. _

*Recorded a half step lower

raise a toast to all of us who are break-ing our backs ev-'ry day.

___ If want-ing the good ___ life is such a crime, then

Lord, put me a-way. ___ Let's do it.

Guitar solo

TOO FAR

Words and Music by
CHAD FISCHER

PROMISED LAND

Words and Music by CHAD FISCHER,
TIM BRIGHT and CHRIS LINK

Spoken: Awe, look at you Cleveland.

Put your hands together for this one.

Yeah, __ yeah, yeah, yeah. _____

POMPEII NIGHTS

Words and Music by CHAD FISCHER,
TIM BRIGHT, ROBERT BURKE
and CHRIS LINK

Hard Rock

We're liv-ing in the king-dom of
Danc-ing with the dev-il in a

rock and roll, ___ it's an em-pi-re of lust, ___ read-y
ring of fire, ___ read-y to e-rupt ___ with mol-

to ex-plode. ___ We're gon-na melt your minds with our
ten de-sire. ___ I found a hot spot that I